HEALTH MATTERS

Autism

Carol
Baldwin

Heinemann Library
Chicago, Illinois

Designed by Patricia Stevenson
Printed and bound in the United States
by Lake Book Manufacturing

07 06 05 04 03
10 9 8 7 6 5 4 3 2 1

Library of Congress Cataloging-in-Publication Data
Baldwin, Carol, 1943–
    Autism / Carol Baldwin.
        p. cm. — (Health matters)
Includes bibliographical references and index.
    ISBN 1-40340-250-7
    1. Autism—Juvenile literature. [1. Autism.
    2. People with mental disabilities.] I. Title.

RC553.A88 B35 2002
616.89'82—dc21

2001007973

Acknowledgments
The author and publishers are grateful to the
following for permission to reproduce copyright
material:

Cover photograph by Michael Newman/Photo Edit

p. 4 IT Stock/Index Stock Imagery/PictureQuest; p.
5 Nance Trueworthy/Stock Boston, Inc.; p. 6 Vecto
Verso/e Stock Photography/PictureQuest; pp. 7, 8
David Woodroffe; p. 9 IFA Bilderteam/eStock
Photography/PictureQuest; p. 10 Laura
Dwight/PhotoEdit/PictureQuest; p. 11 Will and Deni
McIntyre/Photo Researchers Inc.; p. 12 SIU School
of Medicine/Photo Researchers, Inc.; pp. 13, 22 Bob
Daemmrich/Stock Boston, Inc./PictureQuest; p. 14,
21 John Walmsley; p. 15 Felicia
Martinez/PhotoEdit/PictureQuest; p. 16 Walter
Silver/Index Stock Imagery/PictureQuest; p. 17
Mark Azavedo/Heinemann Library; p. 18 Gallo
Images/Corbis; p. 19 Gregg Mancuso/Stock Boston,
Inc.; p. 20 David Woods/Corbis Stock Market; p. 23
Margaret Miller/Photo Researchers, Inc.; p. 24
Najlah Feanny/Stock Boston, Inc./PictureQuest; p.
25 Mark C. Burnett/Photo Researchers, Inc.; p. 26
Bob Daemmrich/Stock Boston, Inc.; p. 27T Michael
Marzelli/Index Stock Imagery/PictureQuest; p. 27B
Temple Grandin; p. 28T Michael Wawro; p. 28B
Jan de Blois

Every effort has been made to contact copyright
holders of any material reproduced in this book.
Any omissions will be rectified in subsequent
printings if notice is given to the publisher.

Some words are shown in bold, **like this.** You can find out what they
mean by looking in the glossary.

Contents

What Is Autism?

Autism is a **condition** that causes people to view and react to the world around them differently than most other people do. It is difficult for people with autism to communicate with others.

Autism affects people's lives in different ways. But most autistic people have problems in four main categories:

◆ **Communication:** They may have problems speaking or listening to other people.

◆ **Social skills:** It may be hard for them to get along with other people and understand their feelings.

◆ Behavior: They may become upset and throw temper tantrums if things happen unexpectedly or if their daily schedule is changed.

◆ Senses: They may be more sensitive and respond more strongly to heat, coldness, and loud noises.

For people with autism, the world is often a confusing place.

4

Kinds of autism

There is a wide range of different types and levels of autism. Some young people with autism have a lot of problems. They almost never talk, and they seem to be in their own world most of the time.

However, most children have more mild autism and go to regular schools. They talk and learn just like you do. They just may have trouble understanding other people at times. They also might have trouble making friends. And they might like being alone more than playing with other children.

A child with autism may not be able to tell whether a classmate is upset or happy.

Asperger syndrome is a kind of autism. Children with Asperger syndrome have fewer problems speaking and learning than other children with autism. They may, however, have difficulty understanding what people mean or how they feel. When you talk to someone, you can usually tell how that person feels by the look on his or her face. People with Asperger syndrome may find it hard to spot and understand signals like these.

Other problems

Some children with autism have other medical problems, too. Children with autism are more likely to have **seizures** than other children are. Seizures can cause unusual body movements and behavior changes.

Some children with autism sometimes injure themselves. This is a behavior that doctors still don't understand. These children may scratch or bite themselves. Or they may bang their heads against a wall over and over again. While this isn't common behavior, it can be a serious problem.

Many children with autism often use their senses of taste and smell to learn about things. Doctors don't know why they do this. But these children must be protected from tasting or smelling things that could hurt them or make them ill.

Doctors are still working to find reasons why autistic children often have other medical problems, too.

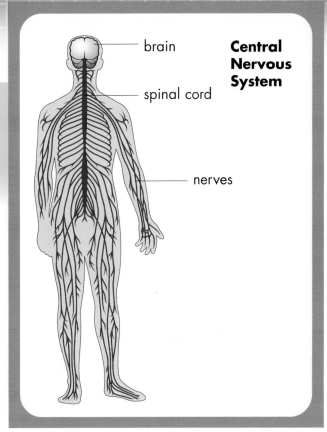

brain

Central Nervous System

spinal cord

nerves

Your brain, spinal cord, and the network of nerves in your body make up your **central nervous system.**

What Causes Autism?

Autism is caused by differences in the way the brains of autistic people work. The parts of the brain that take in information and make sense of it don't work normally in people with autism.

How the brain works

Your brain is the control center of your body. It makes sure that all of the different parts work together correctly. It controls how you think, learn, and feel.

Your brain is connected to the other parts of your body by **nerves.** Messages from all parts of your body travel from nerves to your **spinal cord.** From your spinal cord, which is inside your backbone, messages travel to your brain. Messages also travel in the opposite direction, from your brain to your body.

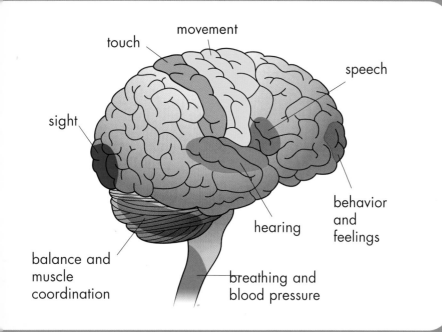

movement
touch
speech
sight
behavior and feelings
hearing
balance and muscle coordination
breathing and blood pressure

Different parts of your brain have different jobs in your body. In a child with autism, the brain works differently than usual.

How autism affects the brain

Your brain is very complicated. It contains over 100 billion **nerve** cells. Each nerve cell has hundreds or thousands of connections to other nerve cells in your brain and body. Different parts of your brain deal with different kinds of messages. Some parts are involved in responding to signals from your **sensory organs.** These parts allow you to see, hear, taste, smell, and touch. Other parts are involved in speaking, moving, thinking, emotions, and memory.

Scientists think that, for some reason, some of the cells and connections in autistic children's brains don't develop in the usual way. In autistic children, the parts of the brain involved with taking in information and figuring out what it means are affected. Parts of the brain that deal with how they think and feel about things are also affected. This explains why autistic children have trouble making sense of the world around them.

Possible causes

Scientists still don't know exactly what causes the differences in the brains of autistic people. But studies have shown some possible causes. For example, in people with autism, less blood than normal flows to certain parts of their brains. People with autism also have fewer numbers of certain kinds of **nerve** cells in their brains.

Doctors also know that having autism can run in families. So a family that has one child with autism is more likely to have a second child with autism. Studies of identical twins also show that if autism occurs in one twin, it is likely to occur in both twins.

Doctors think autism might sometimes be caused by problems a mother had before or during her child's birth. These include the mother having German measles while she was pregnant or the baby not getting enough oxygen during birth.

You probably learned at an early age to be careful when crossing the street. However, a child with autism has a hard time understanding that crossing a street can be dangerous.

Diagnosing Autism

Figuring out if a child has autism can be difficult. Usually a parent is the first person to wonder if something is wrong. Some things a parent might notice in their child include the following:

◆ A child may be old enough to talk, but doesn't. Or a child may simply repeat what is said to him or her, like an echo.

◆ A child may not respond when his or her name is called or look at the person calling. If picked up, a young child might stiffen his or her body and become upset.

◆ A child may behave in unusual and repetitive ways. For example, he or she might constantly spin objects. He or she might constantly rub or scratch certain surfaces like a carpet or a stuffed animal. Or a child might flap his or her hands constantly.

To **diagnose** autism, a doctor has to study what a child has been like from birth. Then they talk about this with the child's parents and caregivers.

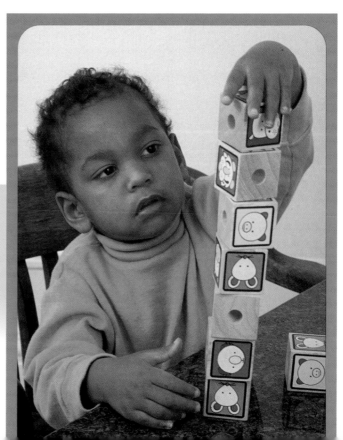

Young children with autism often use toys in unusual ways. For example, they might always arrange their blocks in the same way.

The tests that doctors and specialists use to find out if a child has autism also let them know the child's strengths and weaknesses. This allows them to plan the best ways to help the child.

The doctors also meet with the child. They watch how the child reacts to many different situations. Often doctors and **specialists** work together to figure out what is wrong. They study how the child plays, learns, **communicates,** and behaves to find out if they are autistic.

Autistic savants

About one in ten people with autism have special talents. They are called autistic **savants.** Their talents may include:

- being able to memorize and recall long lists of information

- being able to do calendar calculations. Some savants can tell you what day of the week it was on a date thousands of years ago.

- being able to multiply and divide large numbers in their heads

- being very talented with music, such as being able to play a piece of music after hearing it only once

- being a very talented artist, for example, being able to make a sculpture of an animal after only seeing it on television

Treating Autism

Autism can't be cured. But doctors and special teachers can help children with autism overcome many of their difficulties.

Children need to have certain skills in order to do well in school. They need to be able to **communicate** and work with their classmates. Children with autism have a much harder time learning these things than you did. The earlier a child with autism gets help, the easier it is for him or her to learn these skills. Most children begin to get help before they start school.

In some programs to help young autistic children, specially trained teachers go to the child's home for several hours every day. They work with the child to help him learn basic skills such as naming colors and shapes. They present new skills in a way that the child will find fun and easy to learn. The goal of these programs for preschool children is to help the child learn new skills fast enough to catch up to other children.

The earlier a child with autism gets help for his problems, the more successful he will be when he starts school.

Autistic children often need special help to learn to talk and communicate.

Learning to communicate

Learning how to communicate is an important step for autistic children. If a child can't tell a parent or teacher what he or she needs or wants, it can be very upsetting. **Speech therapists** work with young autistic children to help them learn to talk. Sometimes they start by teaching children to communicate by pointing or using pictures. They might also teach the child how to use **sign language.** Eventually, many children with autism do learn to talk.

To help a child learn to speak, a speech therapist might place several objects on a table. The therapist will point to one of the objects and say its name. Then he or she will ask the child to say its name. This is a first step in learning to talk. Over time, the child learns to say the names of different objects when the therapist points to them. For some autistic children, it takes many hours of work to learn to speak in sentences. But finally, they are able to begin to communicate with others.

Specially trained teachers help autistic children learn social skills, such as how to share their toys.

Learning social skills

For children, **social skills** include such things as playing with toys, sharing toys, and making friends. Unlike most children, these skills do not come naturally to autistic children. Many young children with autism have to be taught how to play with toys. To do this, a parent or teacher will play with a toy themselves, for instance, rolling a car on the ground. Then they'll instruct the child to copy their movements. Eventually, the child is also taught how to share, how to take turns, and how to pretend.

Autistic children need extra help learning how to greet people, wait their turn, and follow directions. Some children also need special help learning skills such as dressing themselves, brushing their teeth, and setting the table. And others need help controlling their tempers and learning how to behave.

14

Throughout the day

For many autistic children, following a strict routine in their daily activities is very important to them. Disruptions or changes to their daily schedule can upset them. For instance, an autistic child may need to eat the same after-school snack at the same time every day. They may become very upset if their parent offers them a different snack.

Sometimes autistic children use activity schedules to help them do everything they need to during the day. An activity schedule is a set of pictures or words that reminds a child to do a series of activities. Activity schedules are usually kept together in a three-ring binder. Each page has pictures or words on it reminding the child to do a series of activities. Young children who can't read can use schedules with pictures. Older children use schedules with words. An after-school activity schedule might include such things as *do math homework, practice piano, have snack, do reading homework,* and *set table for dinner.*

You would probably get bored if you had the same snack every day after school. But some autistic children may get very upset if their after-school snack is changed.

Classmates with Autism

Children who have mild autism can often go to a regular school. However, many children with autism need calmer, more orderly settings. These children often attend special classes in regular schools. Other children go to special schools just for children with autism. Still other autistic children learn at home.

There may be big differences among your classmates with autism. But most children with autism learn to deal quite well with their **condition.** Your classmates with autism probably find it hard to express themselves. They may speak in one tone, so their voices don't go up and down as yours does when you talk. They may have difficulty understanding when and how to ask or answer questions. They also may not understand what people mean when they make certain faces. However, just like you, children with autism go on learning as they grow up.

Autistic students need calm, quiet settings to concentrate on their schoolwork.

16

Common behavior

Classmates with autism might have problems with **social skills** and **communication** skills. In school, social skills include talking, working, and playing with your classmates. Here are some of the behaviors you might notice in a classmate with autism. Not all of your classmates with autism do all of these things, and many stop doing them as they get older.

Many children with autism say they think in pictures, not words. Teachers often use picture books to help these children learn communication skills.

Classmates with autism may:

• talk to you but not listen to what you say

• not always look at people when talking

• sometimes do not seem to care about how other people feel

• talk about one topic all the time

• laugh and giggle at inappropriate times

• not want to play with other children

• join in only if an adult insists on it

• like things to always be the same

• get upset when things in the classroom change

Sensitivity

Your senses include smelling, touching, tasting, seeing, and hearing. They act as a guide to the world around you. But the senses of many children with autism give them wrong or exaggerated messages. For example, an autistic classmate may be very sensitive to touch. He or she might not like the feel of certain kinds of clothing or having someone touch them.

Other classmates might be very sensitive to sound and light. They might be upset by background noises in the classroom. For instance, if someone is mowing grass outside the classroom, they might cover their ears. Some autistic classmates might find bright lights painful.

Still other classmates with autism may be sensitive to tastes and smells. They might not like the taste of many foods. Or they may complain about the smells of food, soap, animals, or people. Some autistic classmates may avoid groups on the playground because the noise is too loud, others touch them, or the smell of other children bothers them.

Some autistic children find that listening to quiet, natural sounds helps them relax and concentrate on their schoolwork.

Classmates with autism may have a special interest in certain classes, such as art. They usually do very well in those classes.

Special interests

Many children with autism have special interests or hobbies that they spend a lot of time doing. Their hobby might be collecting stamps or learning about dogs. Or it could be collecting facts about their favorite music group. These special interests can sometimes cause problems for them. An autistic classmate might find it hard to talk or think about anything else. Sometimes they will focus in strongly on one thing and cannot pay attention to anything else.

However, a special interest doesn't have to be a problem. An autistic classmate can use his or her hobby to help with schoolwork. For example, he or she might read a book about their favorite subject to help with his or her reading skills. And as they grow up, many people with autism get jobs that are connected with their special interests.

Summer camp

Some of your classmates with autism might go to a special camp with other children who have learning problems. Camps with special programs let them learn ways to improve their **social skills** and work on their behavior. The fun part about summer camps is that while campers are learning, they can enjoy all the activities of camp, such as swimming, hiking, and arts and crafts.

Camps for children with autism have a daily schedule that doesn't change. This means there are no surprises for children who like things to be the same. Activities at camp allow them to practice social skills. They also practice skills that will help them do better in school. Your classmate might practice math skills by figuring out his batting average from a baseball game. Or he might read a story about a special interest that he has. These camps can also help an autistic classmate learn how to join in group activities more easily.

Summer camps for children with autism help them improve their social skills and build friendships.

How You Can Help

Autism isn't an illness that can be fixed by taking medicine. Autism is part of who a person is. It affects how he or she thinks and feels. Most of your classmates who have autism work hard to deal with their problems, but they need other people's understanding and support.

Sometimes children with autism might get upset or angry when they don't understand things in class. Specially trained teachers can help these children, but you can help in your own way, too. Sometimes just explaining things in a different way can help your classmate understand a new idea.

The buddy system

In some schools, children with autism have a "buddy." This is a classmate who spends time with them and hangs out with them on the playground. The buddy helps them join in games and explains any rules they might not understand. You might be able to be a buddy to a classmate with autism.

Some children with autism just need someone to explain things to them in a way they can understand.

Fair treatment

Classmates with autism often behave differently than other students. This may make them seem strange to other children who, because of it, might pick on or tease their autistic classmates. No one should have to put up with bullying. If you see someone picking on a classmate who has autism, or anyone else, you should tell a teacher.

Classmates who pick on someone with autism don't understand what autism is. They might think a child with autism doesn't have feelings, so it doesn't matter if they tease him or her. If you have a friend with autism, you know that your friend has feelings. He or she just has a hard time expressing them. You might try explaining this to classmates who tease. Or you might ask your teacher or an autistic friend's parent to talk to your class about autism. This can help correct any wrong ideas your classmates might have.

Just because a child is a little different doesn't mean it's okay to pick on her.

Visiting a Friend with Autism

Everyone likes to go home at the end of the day and relax. This is especially important for a friend who has autism. He or she probably had to make a special effort during the school day to behave the way other people expect. He or she might have been upset because of unexpected changes that happened at school. Maybe your regular teacher was out sick, or maybe the schedule changed because of a field trip. All of these things can upset an autistic friend.

If you go to your friend's house after school to do homework together, you might discover that your friend wants to do things the same way every time. He or she might always want to have an after-school snack first. And your friend might always want to do his or her homework in the same order. As long as you're willing to adjust to the schedule, you can still get all your homework done.

Most children with autism like to keep to a certain schedule. If you're doing your homework with an autistic friend, he may want to do math homework before studying for a spelling test.

If you have dinner at an autistic friend's house, your friend will probably want to sit in his regular chair.

Eating meals

If you stay for dinner, you might notice again that your friend likes to have things the same way. You might find that he or she always likes to eat dinner in exactly the same spot, or sit in a certain chair. Your friend might get very upset if a parent suggests he or she sit somewhere else.

You might also notice that your friend won't eat certain foods. This can sometimes be a problem for the rest of the family. Your friend's older sister might love spaghetti. But if their mother serves it for dinner, your friend might become upset and refuse to eat. He might not like the smell of spaghetti. Or he might say it feels slimy when he eats it. Your friend doesn't mean to upset the family at dinner, but sometimes that happens. If they want to have something he won't eat, his parents might have to make a different meal for him.

Getting along

If you visit a friend who has autism, don't be surprised if your friend doesn't get along with a brother or sister. Your friend's brother or sister may have to deal with behavior that is annoying. For example, they may have to stop playing a board game if your friend is losing because he or she gets very upset. They often find it hard to live with a child who always causes problems.

Children with autism take up a lot of their parents' time. This can also cause problems for your friend's brothers and sisters. They may get upset because their parents pay so much attention to the child with autism. They may think it's unfair that they get in trouble when they do something wrong, but your friend never does. However, they learn to understand that your friend may not realize when he or she is doing something wrong. And eventually they learn to adjust to your friend's autism, just like you can.

Doing something you both enjoy, such as playing a game or watching a video, is a good way to spend time with an autistic friend.

Being friends

Children with autism sometimes have trouble making friends. But once their classmates understand what autism is, making friends becomes a lot easier for them. Remember, having autism doesn't make a child very different from other children. Everybody is a little different in his or her own way. Life would pretty boring if all your friends were exactly alike.

Everyone needs to have friends, whether or not they have autism. These are some tips that can help anyone be a better friend:

- Treat people the same way you want them to treat you.

- Don't say things to hurt people's feelings.

- Tell people when they have done something good or nice.

- Don't lose your temper.

- Be willing to share.

- Don't be afraid to say you're sorry when you do something wrong.

There are many good points about having a friend who has autism. One is that it lets you see the world in a whole new way.

Autism Success Stories

In 2001, Lee Alderman was one of 141 students that graduated from Cardozo High School in Washington, D.C. Two things made the graduation special for him. First, he was the top student in the class. Second, he has mild autism. At the graduation, Lee thanked his mother for everything she had done to help him. He also thanked his teachers and classmates. He said they helped him overcome his

difficulties with schoolwork and **social skills.** Because of his hard work and good grades, he received a scholarship to a college in Maryland.

Dr. Temple Grandin is an animal scientist. She teaches a class in livestock (hogs and cattle) handling at a university. She also designs buildings that house livestock. She says that because

she is autistic, she thinks in pictures. When preparing a design, she can see, in her mind, the whole project at once. In a book about her life, she describes living with autism and tells how she experiences the world differently from other people.

27

Richard Wawro is an autistic **savant** who is a famous artist. Although he was not able to speak well until he was eleven years old, he started drawing when he was only three. When he was six, he went to a children's center where he began to draw with crayons. People were amazed at his talent. Richard can make drawings from scenes he has seen only once on television or in books. Richard is also able to remember exactly when and where he drew each picture. He has sold more than a thousand of his pictures.

Tony DeBlois is a musical savant who is also blind. He began playing the organ when he was only two years old. He now can play fourteen different musical instruments. He also plays many different styles of music. They include jazz, country, and classical music. He received a music scholarship to college and graduated with honors in 1996. He has also made two CDs of his music.

Learning More about Autism

Parents, doctors, and **specialists** know that it's important for children with autism to get help as soon as possible. Because of this, many states now have what are called Early Autism Projects. These programs teach young children the skills they need to be ready to enter school. Many children with autism are helped greatly by these programs.

If you want to learn more about autism, here are some places you can look. Going over the information they offer with a parent or other adult can help you better understand a friend who has autism.

Autism Society of America (ASA)
7910 Woodmont Avenue, Suite 650
Bethesda, MD 20814
301-657-0881

Families for Early Autism Treatment (FEAT)
P.O. Box 255722
Sacramento, CA 95865
916-843-1536

If you have a computer with an Internet connection at school or at home, you can also find many websites with information on autism.

Glossary

Asperger syndrome   type of autism characterized by fewer difficulties with communication, social skills, and behavior

central nervous system   part of the nervous system made up of the brain and the spinal cord

communication   sharing information, such as what you think and how you feel

condition   health problem that a person has for a long time, perhaps for all of his or her life

diagnose   to recognize what illness or condition a person has

nerve   tiny bundle of cells that passes information between different parts of the brain or between the brain and other body parts

savant   person with a special talent or skill

seizure   sudden attack caused by activity in the brain that isn't normal. A seizure might include jerky body movements, loss of consciousness, or unusual behavior.\

sensory organ   body part, such as the eyes, ears, nose, tongue, and skin, that gathers information from surroundings

sign language   system of language in which people use their hands, upper parts of the body, and facial expressions to communicate

social skills   skills needed to get along and communicate with other people. In children, social skills include such things as sharing toys and making friends.

specialist   person who studies and works in a specific area of knowledge

speech therapist   person who is specially trained to help others learn to speak

spinal cord   part of the body that links your brain to nerves all through your body. It is protected by the backbone.

More Books to Read

Edwards, Michele Engel. *Autism*. Farmington Hills, Mich.: Lucent Books, 2001.

Gartenberg, Zachary. *Mori's Story: A Book about a Boy with Autism*. Minneapolis, Minn.: The Lerner Publishing Group, 1988.

Rosenberg, Marcia. *Coping When a Brother or Sister Is Autistic*. New York: The Rosen Publishing Group, 2000.

Index